YOU'VE HAD IT, CHARLIE BROWN

Books by Charles M. Schulz

Peanuts
More Peanuts
Good Grief, More Peanuts!
Good Ol' Charlie Brown
Snoopy
You're Out of Your Mind, Charlie Brown!
But We Love You, Charlie Brown
Peanuts Revisited
Go Fly a Kite, Charlie Brown
Peanuts Every Sunday
It's a Dog's Life, Charlie Brown
You Can't Win, Charlie Brown
Snoopy, Come Home
You Can Do It, Charlie Brown
We're Right Behind You, Charlie Brown
As You Like It, Charlie Brown
Sunday's Fun Day, Charlie Brown
You Need Help, Charlie Brown
Snoopy and the Red Baron
The Unsinkable Charlie Brown
You'll Flip, Charlie Brown
You're Something Else, Charlie Brown
Peanuts Treasury
You're You, Charlie Brown
You've Had It, Charlie Brown

YOU'VE HAD IT, CHARLIE BROWN

A NEW PEANUTS® BOOK

by Charles M. Schulz

HOLT, RINEHART AND WINSTON
New York • Chicago • San Francisco

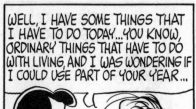

STUPID KID! I JUST HAD THAT CARPET IN THE FRONT HALL CLEANED!

HERE'S THE WORLD-FAMOUS HOCKEY PLAYER WINDING UP FOR ONE OF HIS SPECTACULAR SLAP SHOTS...

POW!

SOME PEOPLE HAVE DOGS WHO BARK TOO MUCH... SOME PEOPLE HAVE DOGS WHO CHASE CHICKENS... SOME PEOPLE HAVE DOGS WHO DIG UP FLOWERS...

"GREAT SHOT!" THANK YOU, STAN.. THANK YOU, BOBBY.. THANK YOU, MAURICE...

WHAT IN THE WORLD ARE YOU DOING?

I'M LOWERING THE PITCHER'S MOUND... ACCORDING TO THE NEW BASEBALL RULES, THE PITCHER'S MOUND MUST BE LOWERED THIS YEAR...

IT SEEMS THAT WE PITCHERS DOMINATED THE GAME TOO MUCH LAST YEAR...

HA HA HA HA HA HA

I KNEW I SHOULDN'T HAVE SAID THAT

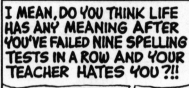

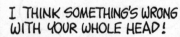

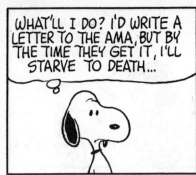

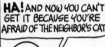

RATS! WHAT A DUMB THING TO DO!

YOU THREW YOUR SUPPER DISH INTO THE NEXT YARD?

HA! AND NOW YOU CAN'T GET IT BECAUSE YOU'RE AFRAID OF THE NEIGHBOR'S CAT

WELL, IT SERVES YOU RIGHT!

OH, GOOD GRIEF HERE IT COMES... "THE LECTURE"

YOU WERE MAD BECAUSE I GAVE YOU CAT FOOD, AND NOW YOUR TEMPER HAS GOTTEN YOU INTO TROUBLE, HASN'T IT?

I CAN'T STAND THESE LECTURES... EVERY TIME YOU DO SOMETHING WRONG, YOU HAVE TO LISTEN TO A LECTURE!

IT JUST DOESN'T PAY TO LOSE YOUR TEMPER.. SELF-CONTROL IS A SIGN OF MATURITY.. TEMPER IS..

LECTURE LECTURE LECTURE

I CAN'T STAND IT! I'D RATHER FACE THAT STUPID CAT THAN ANOTHER LECTURE..

I'LL JUST CLIMB OVER THIS HEDGE, AND GET MY SUPPER DISH BACK!

I'LL JUST GO RIGHT UP TO THAT STUPID CAT, AND SAY, "UNHAND MY SUPPER DISH, YOU STUPID CAT!" AND..

..AND THAT STUPID CAT WILL KILL ME!

I CAN STAND THE LECTURE

JOGGING IS MY THING!

I HAVE A LOT OF QUESTIONS ABOUT LIFE, AND I'M NOT GETTING ANY ANSWERS!

I WANT SOME REAL HONEST-TO-GOODNESS ANSWERS...

I DON'T WANT A LOT OF OPINIONS...I WANT ANSWERS!

WOULD TRUE OR FALSE BE ALL RIGHT?

I WOULD HAVE MADE A GOOD PRAIRIE DOG!

THERE'S A PRAIRIE DOG IN OUR BACK YARD

PRAIRIE DOGS WENT OUT WITH THE COVERED WAGON

LUCY SAYS PRAIRIE DOGS WENT OUT WITH THE COVERED WAGON

WE PRAIRIE DOGS ARE MAKING A COME BACK!

PRAIRIE DOGS ARE MAKING A COME BACK

SMAK!

WE PRAIRIE DOGS ARE VERY AFFECTIONATE

I DON'T UNDERSTAND IT...

EVERY TIME SNOOPY GETS A LETTER FROM LILA, HE BECOMES VERY UPSET.. I DON'T EVEN KNOW WHAT LILA LOOKS LIKE..ONE TIME SHE CAME TO SEE HIM, AND HE RAN AND HID...

AND NOW WHAT HAPPENS? SHE WRITES TO HIM AGAIN, AND HE SUDDENLY TAKES OFF TO SEE HER! WHY? I DON'T UNDERSTAND IT!

LILA NEEDS ME!

WOW! WHAT A BIG HOSPITAL!

IF ANY OF THE NURSES CATCH ME, THEY'LL KILL ME... THEY HATE BEAGLES IN HOSPITALS...

LILA?

SNOOPY!!

HI, SWEETIE!

YOU BOUGHT SNOOPY IN THE MONTH OF OCTOBER, RIGHT?

ACCORDING TO THE RECORDS AT THE DAISY HILL PUPPY FARM, SNOOPY WAS BOUGHT BY ANOTHER FAMILY IN AUGUST...THIS FAMILY HAD A LITTLE GIRL NAMED LILA...

SNOOPY AND LILA LOVED EACH OTHER VERY MUCH, BUT THEY LIVED IN AN APARTMENT, AND THE FAMILY DECIDED THEY JUST COULDN'T KEEP SNOOPY SO THEY RETURNED HIM...

YOU GOT A USED DOG, CHARLIE BROWN!

NOW, I SEE WHY THOSE LETTERS FROM LILA WOULD UPSET SNOOPY SO MUCH

SURE, HE WAS TRYING TO FORGET HER, BUT WHEN HE FOUND OUT SHE WAS IN THE HOSPITAL, HE RAN OFF TO SEE HER...

I'LL BET HE WISHES HE WAS STILL HER DOG INSTEAD OF MINE...

I DOUBT IT, CHARLIE BROWN.. HE WOULDN'T HAVE BEEN HAPPY IN AN APARTMENT

HERE'S THE WORLD WAR I FLYING ACE ZOOMING THROUGH THE AIR IN HIS SOPWITH CAMEL!

SCHULZ

LOOK INTO MY EYES, AND TELL ME I'M BEAUTIFUL...

WHAT?

HE TALKS!

YOU DISLIKE ME, DON'T YOU?

YOU HATE ME...YOU DETEST ME...YOU LOATHE ME...YOU ABHOR ME...YOU DESPISE ME..

I'VE NEVER SAID THAT I DESPISE YOU

REALLY?

LET'S WORK OUR WAY BACKWARD THROUGH THAT LIST...

MY PIANO IS GONE

NOW MAYBE YOU'LL PAY SOME ATTENTION TO **ME**!

I DON'T UNDERSTAND YOU

ALL I WANT IS FOR YOU TO NOTICE ME ONCE IN A WHILE...IS THAT ASKING SO MUCH?

MY PIANO IS GONE

MAYBE I SHOULD HAVE THROWN **HIM** UP INTO THE TREE!

I'M ORDERING A NEW PIANO FROM THE "ACE PIANO COMPANY"

THEY HAVE A SPECIAL ON...WITH EVERY TOY PIANO YOU BUY, YOU GET A PHOTOGRAPH OF JOE GARAGIOLA

I SUPPOSE YOUR OLD PIANO WAS COVERED BY INSURANCE...

HOW DO YOU EXPLAIN TO AN INSURANCE COMPANY THAT YOUR PIANO WAS EATEN BY A TREE?

RING!!

HELLO?

JUST A MOMENT, PLEASE... I'LL CALL HIM..

TELEPHONE!

WHO COULD BE CALLING ME? IT'S PROBABLY BAD NEWS..

MAYBE SOMEONE'S SICK OR MAYBE THERE WAS A FIRE OR A FLOOD OR SOMETHING..

MAYBE IT ISN'T BAD NEWS...

MAYBE IT'S JOE GARAGIOLA CALLING ME, OR BOBBY HULL OR KERMIT ZARLEY.....

MAYBE IT'S SOMEONE FROM NASA ...THEY'RE PROBABLY HAVING TROUBLE AND NEED MY ADVICE AGAIN..

HE SAYS TO TELL YOU HE HAS ALL THE MAGAZINES HE WANTS!

!

I WONDER WHY JOE GARAGIOLA NEVER CALLS ME...

I'VE BEEN THINKING ABOUT SOMETHING...

IN THE BIG LEAGUES, WHEN A TEAM GETS A RALLY STARTED, SOMEONE BLOWS A TRUMPET AND EVERYONE YELLS, "CHARGE!!"

DO YOU THINK WE COULD DO THAT, CHARLIE BROWN?

I DON'T KNOW...WE'VE NEVER HAD A RALLY...

TIME OUT....THERE'S A BUG CROSSING THE INFIELD...

CURSE THIS STUPID WAR! CURSE YOU, TOO, RED BARON!

IT IS DAWN...

HERE'S THE WORLD WAR I FLYING ACE WALKING OUT TO HIS SOPWITH CAMEL..

HE WAVES A CHEERY "GOOD MORNING" TO HIS GROUND CREW... THESE ARE GOOD LADS..

THIS IS A VERY DANGEROUS MISSION... BUT, ALAS...AREN'T THEY ALL? WHAT MUST BE DONE, MUST BE DONE! WHAT COURAGE! WHAT FORTITUDE!

BEFORE I TAKE OFF, MY FAITHFUL GROUND CREW GATHERS ABOUT ME BIDDING FAREWELL.. THEY ARE VERY DISTURBED.. SOME FEEL THAT PERHAPS WE SHALL NEVER SEE EACH OTHER AGAIN...

WHAT AN EMOTIONAL MOMENT! THROATS TIGHTEN, AND TEARS WELL IN OUR EYES...

IS IT POSSIBLE THAT THIS COULD BE MY FINAL MISSION? THAT I SHALL NEVER RETURN? THAT THIS IS THE END?

FORGET IT!

SCHULZ

WHAT'S THE DATE TODAY?

SEPTEMBER NINTH

IT'S NOT CHRISTMAS YET?

I WISH OUR SCHOOL HAD A CAFETERIA..

IT WOULD GIVE ME A BETTER CHANCE TO MEET THAT LITTLE RED-HAIRED GIRL...

I'D SAY, "HELLO, LITTLE RED-HAIRED GIRL... MAY I TREAT YOU TO LUNCH TODAY?"

WHY NOT JUST ASK HER TO BROWN-BAG IT?

WHERE SHALL WE SIT?

RIGHT OVER THERE

YES, MA'AM? THE BACK ROW? WHY DID I TAKE A SEAT IN THE BACK ROW?

YES, MA'AM, I KNOW THERE ARE SEATS IN THE FRONT ROW... I WAS MERELY OBEYING THE BIBLICAL ADMONITION...

IN THE FOURTEENTH CHAPTER OF LUKE, BEGINNING WITH THE TENTH VERSE, WE READ, "WHEN YOU ARE INVITED, GO AND SIT IN THE LOWEST PLACE SO THAT WHEN YOUR HOST COMES HE MAY SAY TO YOU, 'FRIEND, GO UP HIGHER';"

"..EVERY ONE WHO EXALTS HIMSELF WILL BE HUMBLED, AND HE WHO HUMBLES HIMSELF WILL BE EXALTED."

YES, MA'AM..

MISS OTHMAR ISN'T MUCH FOR BIBLICAL ADMONITIONS...

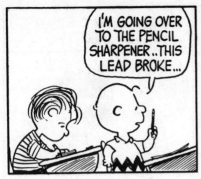

I'M GOING OVER TO THE PENCIL SHARPENER..THIS LEAD BROKE...

ACTUALLY, IT ISN'T LEAD AT ALL.. IT'S A COMBINATION OF BAVARIAN CLAY AND MADAGASCAR GRAPHITE

YOU'RE THE ONLY PERSON I KNOW WHO CAN TAKE THE JOY OUT OF SHARPENING A PENCIL!

MISS OTHMAR?

WOULD YOU PLEASE REPEAT OUR HOMEWORK ASSIGNMENT?

"WRITE A TWO-PAGE THEME ON WHAT WE DID THIS SUMMER"

HOW DO YOU TEACHERS KEEP COMING UP WITH THESE GREAT NEW IDEAS?

POOR MISS OTHMAR... IT'S RAINING, AND SHE'S ON STRIKE

I'M BRINGING HER SOME SOUP...

THIS WILL BE JUST WHAT SHE NEEDS...

..A BOWL OF RAIN!

THE TEACHERS ARE STILL ON STRIKE, I SEE..

YES, AND MISS OTHMAR LOOKS TIRED..SHE'S BEEN CARRYING THAT SIGN FOR...

SHE'S FALLEN TO HER KNEES!!

WHAT'S GOING ON?

MISS OTHMAR FELL, AND LINUS RUSHED OVER AND PICKED UP HER SIGN!

THAT STUPID BLOCKHEAD... HE'S BECOME **INVOLVED**!

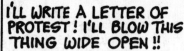

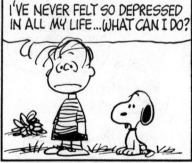

CHARLIE BROWNNNN ♪♫

I CAN'T BELIEVE IT...SHE MUST THINK I'M THE MOST STUPID PERSON ALIVE...

COME ON, CHARLIE BROWN..I'LL HOLD THE BALL, AND YOU KICK IT...

HOLD IT? **HA!** THAT'S A LAUGH! YOU'LL PULL IT AWAY, AND I'LL KILL MYSELF!

WHY, CHARLIE BROWN, HOW CAN YOU SAY THAT? DON'T I HAVE A FACE YOU CAN TRUST? DON'T I HAVE AN INNOCENT LOOK ABOUT ME?

LOOK AT THE INNOCENCE IN MY EYES...

SHE'S RIGHT... IF A GIRL HAS INNOCENT-LOOKING EYES, YOU SIMPLY HAVE TO TRUST HER...

THIS TIME I'M GONNA KICK THAT FOOTBALL CLEAR TO THE MOON!

AAUGH

WHAM!

WHAT YOU HAVE LEARNED HERE TODAY, CHARLIE BROWN, WILL BE OF IMMEASURABLE VALUE TO YOU FOR MANY YEARS TO COME

SIGH!

SCHULZ

THIS IS THE SORT OF DREARY FALL RAIN THAT MAKES YOU WANT TO SIT INSIDE ALL DAY, AND STARE OUT THE WINDOW, AND DRINK TEA AND PLAY SAD SONGS ON THE STEREO

SO WHY AM I LYING HERE?

MY GRAMMA AND I HAVE BEEN HAVING A PHILOSOPHICAL ARGUMENT

SHE THINKS OUR GENERATION IS SPOILED AND UNGRATEFUL...

SHE SAYS THAT AS SOON AS A KID HAS HIS EIGHTEENTH BIRTHDAY, HE SHOULD BE KICKED OUT INTO THE WORLD!

EVEN IF IT'S A SUNDAY?

ANYONE WHO WOULD SIT AROUND BY HIMSELF MAKING FUNNY FACES MUST BE CRAZY

WHAT ELSE IS THERE TO DO ON A SATURDAY AFTERNOON WHEN YOUR GIRL FRIEND HAS LEFT YOU, YOUR TV SET IS BROKEN AND YOUR JOGGING SUIT IS IN THE WASH?

I FEEL DEPRESSED

IT'S RAINING OUTSIDE AND THE WORLD REEKS OF DESPAIR..

EVEN MY COLD CEREAL DOTH TASTE LIKE WORMWOOD..

HOW DEPRESSED CAN YOU GET?

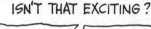

I'M DRAWING A ROW OF TREES, AND I'M GOING TO COLOR THEM GREEN

THAT'S NOT ART

I'LL PUT A LAKE IN FRONT OF THE TREES

THAT STILL WON'T MAKE IT ART

AND BY THE LAKE I'LL DRAW A TINY LOG CABIN

THAT'S NOT ENOUGH... YOU NEED A WATERFALL AND A SUNSET...SHOW THE SUN GOING DOWN SORT OF ORANGEY, AND PUT SOME RED STREAKS IN THE SKY, AND HAVE SOME SMOKE COMING OUT OF THE CHIMNEY

NOW PUT IN SOME MORE TREES...MAKE IT A FOREST... AND HAVE A DEER STANDING BY THE WATERFALL... THAT'S RIGHT...

NOW YOU HAVE TREES, A LAKE, A LOG CABIN, A WATERFALL, A DEER AND A SUNSET...

THAT'S ART!

SOMETIMES IT TAKES A LAYMAN TO SET THESE PEOPLE STRAIGHT

JUST WHAT I THOUGHT

I KNEW IT WOULD HAPPEN SOONER OR LATER...

THEY'VE RUN OUT OF SNOWFLAKES!

WOULD IT OFFEND YOU IF SOMEONE HIT YOU WITH A SNOWBALL, CHARLIE BROWN?

OFFEND ME? NO, I DON'T THINK SO.. IT MIGHT STUN ME OR HURT ME OR SOMETHING LIKE THAT, BUT I DON'T THINK IT WOULD OFFEND ME...

POW!

I'M GLAD I HAVEN'T OFFENDED YOU, CHARLIE BROWN!

AH,HA!!

CAUGHT YOU IN THE ACT, DIDN'T I?

I WANT TO SEE THAT SNOWBALL TAKEN APART SNOWFLAKE BY SNOWFLAKE, AND I WANT TO SEE IT TAKEN APART **NOW**!

NO CHUNKS! NO PIECES! JUST SNOWFLAKES! ONE SNOWFLAKE AT A TIME!

NO PIECES! NO CHUNKS! JUST ONE SNOWFLAKE AT A TIME!

HAVE YOU EVER TRIED TO DISMANTLE A SNOWBALL?

"THE TERROR OF THE ICE"!

HERE'S THE WORLD FAMOUS HOCKEY PLAYER... AS HE SKATES OUT ONTO THE ICE, THE OPPOSING GOALIE BEGINS TO SHAKE WITH FEAR...

HERE'S THE WORLD FAMOUS HOCKEY PLAYER MOVING THE PUCK UP THE ICE...

HE SHOOTS!

IT'S A GOAL!

ONCE AGAIN HE PICKS UP THE PUCK AND MOVES OVER THE BLUE LINE..

HE FLIPS A BACKHAND SHOT..

ANOTHER GOAL!

HE PICKS UP THE PUCK IN CENTER ICE..ACROSS THE BLUE LINE...DOWN THE LEFT SIDE...

IT'S IN!!

I SCORED THREE GOALS WHILE THEY WERE PLAYING THE NATIONAL ANTHEM!

TOMORROW IS BEETHOVEN'S BIRTHDAY..

I HAVE AN IDEA FOR A GREAT PARTY!

WE'LL INVITE AN EQUAL NUMBER OF BOYS AND GIRLS, SEE, AND EACH BOY WILL BRING A GIRL A NICE PRESENT...

AT THE APPOINTED TIME, EACH GIRL WILL OPEN HER PRESENT, AND THEN EACH GIRL WILL GIVE EACH BOY A WARM HUG AND A KISS!

TOMORROW IS BEETHOVEN'S BIRTHDAY..

I SHALL CELEBRATE HIS BIRTHDAY BY PLAYING HIS SONATA IN A FLAT MAJOR, OPUS 110, AND SITTING IN SILENT MEDITATION FOR ONE MINUTE...BY MYSELF!

TOMORROW IS MONDAY..

ICE SKATING IS A GOOD WAY TO MEET GIRLS!

PEGGY FLEMING AND I USED TO SKATE TOGETHER QUITE OFTEN...

...BEFORE I BECAME BIG-TIME!

HE'S A GOOD SKATER, BUT HE'S THE FUNNIEST LOOKING KID I'VE EVER SEEN!

FIRST WE'LL ENTER THE UNITED STATES FIGURE SKATING CHAMPIONSHIPS IN SEATTLE..

THEN WE'LL GO ON TO THE NORTH AMERICAN IN OAKLAND AND FROM THERE TO THE WORLD'S IN COLORADO..

I CAN SEE IT NOW... TROPHIES, ACCLAIM..

..COLD FEET!

WHEN ARE YOU LEAVING FOR OAKLAND?

OAKLAND?! WHO SAID ANYTHING ABOUT LEAVING FOR OAKLAND?

SNOOPY'S COUNTING ON YOU TO SKATE WITH HIM THERE IN THE NORTH AMERICAN CHAMPIONSHIPS...

HE IS?

GEE, CHUCK, I DON'T EVEN KNOW WHERE OAKLAND IS..

I LOOKED IT UP.. IT'S ABOUT FIFTY MILES FROM PETALUMA

PETALUMA?

LOOK, SNOOPY, LET'S FACE IT... I CAN'T GO TO OAKLAND..

I APPRECIATE YOUR WANTING ME TO SKATE WITH YOU IN THE CHAMPIONSHIPS, BUT I JUST CAN'T GO...I'M SORRY...LET'S JUST SAY IT WAS FUN, AND, "SO LONG"...OKAY?

SHE DIDN'T EVEN KISS ME ON THE NOSE!

IS IT CHRISTMAS YET?

FOUR MORE DAYS

HOW COME IT TAKES SO LONG?

CHRISTMAS IS ON TOP OF A STEEP HILL, AND THE CLOSER YOU GET TO IT, THE STEEPER THE HILL IS!

CHRISTMAS IS ON TOP OF A STEEP HILL!

"NOT A CREATURE WAS STIRRING... NOT EVEN A MOUSE"

REMEMBER, IF I DON'T GET SOMETHING QUITE RIGHT, LET ME KNOW...

"THE STOCKINGS WERE HUNG BY THE CHIMNEY WITH CARE.. IN HOPE THAT JACK NICKLAUS SOON WOULD BE THERE"

I ALMOST HATE TO BRING THIS UP...